D0425873

The CEO'S TIME MACHINE

Story by: Geoff Thatcher
Illustrations by: Zoe Thatcher

Casa Flamingo Literary Arts
Nashville, TN

The CEO's Time Machine
Copyright © 2020 by Creative Principals, Inc.
Printed and bound in Nashville, Tennessee, U.S.A.
All rights reserved. No part of this book may be reproduced or
transmitted in any form or by any means, electronic or mechanical, without
prior written permission from the author (gthatcher@creativeprincipals.com).
Reviewers may quote brief passages in a review to be printed in a magazine,
newspaper or on the Web without written permission.

First printing
ISBN: 978-0-9967504-7-9
Library of Congress Control Number (LCCN): 2020936189
Page and text design: Carrie O'Neal
Editor: Callie Stoker, The Manuscript Doctor
Publisher: Tim O'Brien, Casa Flamingo Literary Arts

Distribution: Ingram Global Publisher Services
For additional copies of *The CEO's Time Machine*,
ask your local bookseller to order or visit www.amazon.com.

Dedicated to our muse.

Forty years ago, I set out on a mission to convince business leaders that history isn't just about the past. It's about transforming the future. Applying a methodology called Start with the Future and Work Back,™ I've been privileged to assist many of the world's most competitive organizations in prioritizing initiatives critical to their future success and then systematically working back into their history to pull forward the authentic content that drives employee engagement and innovation.

Over the past few years, I've been fortunate to get to know Geoff Thatcher, personally and professionally, as we worked together on several transformative global exhibitions and events. Upon reading the draft manuscript of *The CEO's Time Machine* that Geoff was kind enough to share, a chill ran up my spine. How had he discovered and so articulately expressed what I had intrinsically sensed, over 40 years of interacting with business founders and CEOs, to be at the core of their success? And, as a fellow creative spirit, I thought to myself: "Gosh. I wish I'd written that."

In *The CEO's Time Machine*, Geoff draws upon his skills as a masterful storyteller and experience designer to guide his readers through a genuine inventory of history to ultimately arrive at a singular moment of insight shared by generations of legendary leaders.

Geoff's storytelling is elegantly simple and profoundly complex. His message is both timely and timeless. And the imaginative craft-like illustrations by Zoe Thatcher complement and embed the narrative to the mind's eye. No matter where you are on your life's journey, I'm confident that you'll experience an "aha moment" in *The CEO's Time Machine*.

Bruce Weindruch
Founder & CEO, History Factory
Author, *Start with the Future and Work Back:*
A Heritage Management Manifesto

CHAPTER 1: THE GARAGE

As the garage door slowly rolled open, she could barely contain her excitement. As the Chief Operating Officer of the world's fastest growing and most innovative company, she was about to become CEO.

And she knew the secret to her future success could be found inside this garage.

She was nervous. In fact, she hadn't been this nervous since the CEO plucked her out of the company's industrial design lab and elevated her to his senior team. At the time, he simply told her, "I've seen your potential and know you will accomplish amazing things—not just for this company or yourself, but for the world."

She believed him.

And why wouldn't she?

Her boss was a visionary.

The secret to his groundbreaking moves were rumored to be inside a locked garage behind one of his company's R&D labs. In fact, the only person in this multi-billion dollar corporation who had a key to this garage was the CEO. That's the way it always had been, and everyone knew that's the way it would always be.

But now, here she was standing next to the CEO as the garage door opened.

"Don't get too excited," he said with a smile. "You are ready to lead this company, and there's just one final thing I need to share with you."

Why, she wondered, was there so much secrecy around the contents inside this garage?

Fifteen years earlier, there had been a lot of activity in this garage when the CEO first took over. At the time, the company was losing market share, laying off employees and struggling to find its place. People wondered if the company would even survive. Outside of this garage, trucks dropped off large crates late at night. Contractors installed enough power and cooling to run a small factory. One janitor reportedly saw something that looked like an F-22 cockpit rolling into the garage. Another employee swore he heard loud rock 'n roll music and saw bright lights flashing as the garage's door opened briefly to let in a contractor. Someone swore they heard horses and gunfire once.

While everyone in the company knew about the garage, the CEO never talked about it—and no one dared ask him about it either. When the CEO fired his first CFO, it was rumored to be over his secret spending on the garage. One story said that the CEO paid for everything inside the garage out of his own pocket to avoid the preying eyes of his board of directors.

Other than the CEO, the only people who had been inside the garage were a small group of mysterious outside contractors who worked directly for the Chief Executive Officer. Word had it that an attorney in the legal department told her assistant that the contract and NDA signed by these contractors was both the most lucrative and punishing document she'd ever seen. When the list of contractors somehow leaked and was published in a blog founded by a former business editor at *Forbes*, not even the blogger could make sense of it.

What's the world's most visionary CEO doing inside a garage at his company's headquarters with a Quantum Physicist, Formula 1 Engineer, Librarian, Astrodynamicist, Professional Poker Player, Gamer, Professor of Divinity, Cosmetologist, Sound Engineer, Machinist, ex-Navy Seal, Hacker, Fashion Designer, and F-22 Test Pilot?

While none of these world-renowned experts would talk to the blogger or even admit that they had met the CEO, let alone stepped inside his mysterious garage, one former employee did speak anonymously about the speculation inside the company.

"They are either in that garage drinking Scotch or they're building something. Hell, maybe he's already built something. How else can you explain it?"

With the CEO's unprecedented track record over the last decade, people were bound to wonder how he did it. The stock had soared far beyond even the most bullish projections. His company didn't just dominate markets, it created new ones. His employees believed they were shaping the future. Despite what some considered to be risky bets, the company succeeded. Everyone, including the blogger, wanted to know this CEO's secret.

As the anonymous tipster we talked with proclaimed, "the answer is inside that garage!" When pressed, this former executive refused to speculate further. "If I say what I really think, everyone will think I'm crazy."

The CEO was happy to let people speculate.

Some said it was simply the world's most expensive man cave. Others argued it was a 21st Century think tank for a modern CEO. Some said it was a secret fraternity or club where members would spend hours inside talking about the future. Still others said the CEO had a secret control room inside where he somehow analyzed data on both his company and the competition.

"What do you think Wilbur Wright would tell you if you went back in time?" the CEO asked his soon-to-be replacement as they stood outside the garage.

"Wilbur Wright?"

"Yes," he responded, "what would you ask Wilbur, or Orville for that matter, if you could go back to 1903?"

The COO's heart leapt as she thought about the insane possiblity of what might be inside the garage.

It can't be…

"I think I'd rather talk to the future me 20 years from now," the COO suggested with a nervous chuckle.

"You'd like to travel into the future, would you?"

The COO nodded.

<u>With a mischievous grin on his face, the CEO then began to walk inside the garage</u> while turning back to his protégé, "sure thing, but let's go talk to Wilbur first, shall we?"

As she followed him inside, the garage door closed.

She expected to walk right into a large, open space with an odd-looking machine sitting beneath the rafters. Yes, she was hoping to immediately see the CEO's time machine, but instead she found herself walking down a long and winding hallway lined with thousands of books, trinkets, artifacts, memorabilia and quite simply junk.

It was cool junk to be sure, and in the first few steps she noticed shelves stuffed full of old auto parts. As an industrial designer, she knew more than a little about automobile design and could recognize most of the parts. However, she was no mechanic, and what she saw before her on the shelves was something out of her uncle's old auto repair shop on the outskirts of Bakersfield, California. Littered along these shelves were batteries, spark plugs, small motors, wires, old car radios and boxes full of old parts.

She stood in the hallway and tried to remember everything she could from her college class on automobile design. She immediately noticed two odd things about this collection of parts. First, there were no modern auto parts. Everything looked like it was from the 20th Century. Second, every part looked, as far as she could tell, like it was made by DELCO.

Hanging down from the ceiling over this junk was a big DELCO Battery sign from the 1920's. As she looked around, she saw other DELCO signs and packaging from the 1930's, 40's, 50's, 60's, 70's and so on.

Next to one of the old DELCO radios, she saw an 8-track tape. It was the album *Tattoo You* by The Rolling Stones. Its aged red cover design featured a young man with Maori tattoos across his face.

"Oh my," she said to the CEO, while picking the large tape up, "my uncle used to have a huge collection of 8-track tapes."

The CEO turned and smiled while motioning to her to put the tape in one of the radios on the shelf.

"They work?"

"Well, that one does," he nodded while pointing.

She put the 8-track tape in the radio and track 1 immediately started playing...

If you start me up

She wasn't a huge Mick Jagger fan, but she certainly was beginning to grasp the symbolism of the junk around her. There on the shelf was a box for a DELCO Remy V-8 Distributor Cap for a 1955 Corvette. And right next to that box was an old hunk of metal with wires coming out of it. While she was no expert in automobiles, it looked to her like some type of electric starter.

The CEO smiled as he noticed his protégé clearly surprised by what she saw around her. "It's a DELCO distributor," he said. "It routes high voltage from the coil to the spark plugs to fire the engine."

She nodded, while slightly bouncing her head up and down to the music. Inside, she was both puzzled and delighted by the CEO's collection of junk.

Another shelf caught her attention and she stepped forward while the music kept playing. This section of hallway was dedicated to old Cadillacs. The shelves were lined with toy models of every Cadillac from the original 1902 Model A Runabout up through the 1940's. A big poster hung on the wall featuring what looked like one of the earliest models. The poster showed the front of the automobile with one simple tagline:

The Car That Has No Crank

"That," the CEO said, "is the 1912 Cadillac Model 30."

She nodded while reading the words on the poster.

"Yeah, the 1912 Cadillac was the first car with an electric self-starter," he said. While looking back at the DELCO sign, he continued, "the starter was actually made by—surprise—DELCO. The Cadillac won the Dewar Trophy from the Royal Automobile Club of London because it eliminated the need for the hand-crank."

"Believe it or not, those cranks were quite dangerous as they had a tendency to snap back. The electric self-starter revolutionized the industry and opened up a huge new market for automakers."

She looked at her boss and said, "women."

He nodded and then kept walking down the hallway, happy with himself for picking such a smart successor.

The COO followed while trying to fully understand why a CEO with a time machine would bother to collect all of this stuff.

Next, they turned a corner and walked through shelves lined from top to bottom with brass and cast iron, antique cash registers.

"These are amazing," she said to the CEO as she stepped closer to look at the intricate patterns on some of the machines. While the floral patterns and fleur-de-lis on many of the machines were beautiful, her favorite was a rather baroque-looking brass register with a cash drawer featuring a gargoyle.

It didn't take her long to notice something that every register had in common. She looked to the CEO and put her hand on one of the cranks on the side of the register with the gargoyle.

"Coincidence?" she asked while turning the crank.

The gargoyle jumped out as the drawer opened and the CEO laughed. "Well, no one ever died from cranking a cash register, but yes, there is a connection. The man who invented the electric motor for the cash register at NCR was also the man who invented the electric starter for the automobile."

She racked her brain trying to remember her automotive history.

"Kettering?"

It was a guess and she only knew the name because a college friend had gotten treatment at the Memorial Sloan Kettering Cancer Center in New York City. She had Googled the name of the Center when visiting and saw something online about its donors being GM executives.

The CEO nodded while brimming from ear to ear, his confidence in her confirmed with every step they took further into his garage. "Yes, Charles Kettering. Do you know much about him?"

"It was a guess," she admitted.

"Well, it was a good one," he responded. "Charles Kettering was an amazing inventor and leader. After joining the National Cash Register Company in the early 1900's, he invented the first electrical cash

register that could be opened with a touch of a button. Seeing the potential, he formed the Dayton Engineering Laboratories Company."

"DELCO," she interrupted.

"Yes, DELCO. Kettering and his team created the first self-starting automobile motor with a key. And that 1912 Cadillac Model 30 was the first. He truly was an amazing inventor. Over his career, Kettering invented quick-drying automotive paint, shock absorbers, safety glass, the automatic transmission, the first synthetic aviation fuel, and Freon for refrigerators and air conditioners. And that's just a few inventions that came out of Dayton, Ohio."

"So," she asked while trying to understand the bigger story, "at the same time Kettering was inventing the self-starting automobile engine, the Wright Brothers were literally down the street inventing airplanes?"

The CEO nodded while walking further down the hallway to a large map on the wall of Montgomery County, Ohio from 1910. "Dayton was the Silicon Valley of the early 1900's," he said while pointing to the map.

"Well," she chuckled, "it's not now."

"No, it's not," he said. "The free market isn't always kind to innovators."

The COO nodded solemnly, knowing now that this trip inside her CEO's garage wasn't just for playing classic rock on old radios.

Not profiting from your innovations truly would make a grown man cry, she thought while still listening to the music of The Rolling Stones on that old 8-track.

"I think I'd cry too if I had a complete monopoly on aviation in 1905 and 10 years later was completely out of the business," the CEO said while picking up David McCullough's book *The Wright Brothers* on the shelf next to the map of Ohio's Montgomery County. He opened the book up to a tabbed page and read, "'We have been compelled to spend our time on business matters', oh, by the way, this is Wilbur writing to a friend about their patent wars. 'When we think what we might have accomplished if we had been able to devote this time to experiments, we feel very sad, but it is always easier to deal with things than with men.'"

"So," the COO said with a smile, "I guess the lesson is to stop dealing with men."

The CEO laughed and then picked up another book called *The Wright Company*. "Now, this is Wilbur again in 1907. 'I want the business built up so as to get the greatest amount of money with as little work. Sell (a) few machines at a big profit, so that we can close out.'"

He then slammed the book shut and put it back on the shelf.

The CEO looked around at all of the stuff he had collected in the hallway. Eyeing the executive that would soon take over his company, he walked down the hallway a few more steps to a shelf that featured hundreds of model airplanes. <u>He gently picked up the 1903 Wright Flyer in one hand and the Lockheed Constellation in the other.</u>

"Wilbur's brother Orville was the first man to fly in 1903. Forty-one years later near the end of World War II, Orville took his last flight in the brand new Lockheed Constellation."

"That's quite a leap," she said.

"His pilot?"

After a short pause, the CEO answered his own question, "Howard Hughes."

The COO now looked at her mentor and leader with her eyes wide open. Her mind was full of questions.

What lies beyond this hallway? What other secrets are inside this garage? What lessons does he want me to learn? How can I ever replace him? What if I fight stupid legal battles instead of innovating? What if I allow politics to get in the way of progress? Will I be able to make the same connections Kettering did? Will I be able to recruit engineers as bright as Kettering? What new markets can we create? How can I avoid losing the markets we've already created? What if I fail?

"I know what people think I have inside this garage," the CEO confessed. "But what they don't know is that if you are going to travel back in time, you first have to do your homework."

And with that, the CEO put the two model airplanes back on the shelf, turned, and walked around the corner.

The COO wasn't sure if she should follow until she heard a voice calling out to her, "are you coming?"

As she followed the CEO down the curving hallway, she continued noticing the strange collection of artifacts, technology, memorabilia, books and other junk. One section was devoted to Disneyland and theme park memorabilia. Another to Apple computers, including iconic models like the original Mac and iPod. And still another to old televisions, including models she had never heard of before, like a large 1951 Motorola.

While she was sure there were more great stories and lessons to be told, the CEO kept walking at a brisk pace. Eventually, the hallway opened up into a large circular room. For a moment, the COO just stood there dumbstruck, trying to take it all in.

"What is this," she chuckled, "Las Vegas?"

The CEO just smiled while his protégé took it all in.

The room resembled a rotunda. It was a perfect circle and formed a dome at the top. In the middle of the room was a 12-foot tall Roman sculpture, but with an eclectic modern twist. Yes, it was made of marble, but there were also wires, cables, steel and other modern aesthetics worked into the design. She immediately noticed that the sculpture had two faces, one facing the hallway they had just come from, and the other pointing the opposite direction. Over the head of this giant Roman sculpture was a series of LED screens arching from the middle down around the room.

"Those look familiar," she said while pointing at the screens. Each screen displayed the latest company metrics from all around the world. In fact, one of her key projects as COO was overseeing a company-wide dashboard and control room that put all the important data about the company on these easy-to-digest screens.

"Look," she said, "sales in EMEA just came in." Without waiting for a response, she continued, "you know, I've been telling our GMs that they need to work more closely with…"

"Let's not talk about the past," he interrupted. "Don't misunderstand me," he said, trying to cheer up the COO. Like anyone, she hated to be cut off mid-sentence. "As you can tell from what you've seen so far, I care a great deal about the past. I collect those

historical artifacts you just saw because I never want to forget the lessons of those who went before us. Here on these screens, we can learn so much from the latest data about our business. That's why we collect the data. That's why I put you in charge of building this amazing system. But the minute this data hits the screens, it's already old. It really doesn't represent the present."

She nodded.

"No, let's talk about the one place that doesn't require a time machine to visit," he said with a wink while turning in a circle around the sculpture and pointing to the other features of this beautifully strange rotunda.

"The present," she said while wondering what was behind the eight doors ringing the edge of the rotunda.

"First, let me introduce you to my friend here." With his hands now high in the air, as if he was giving a tour to 30 people, he announced, "this is the Roman god Janus."

"Well, that explains the doors," she said.

"Yes," he responded with an always approving nod.

"The Roman god of doors and beginnings, with one face looking back into the past to discover his mistakes and enjoy his successes, and the other face looking forward to the future while making plans, and resolutions, for the new year."

"January," she said with a smile.

"January," he responded.

"I had no idea you were such a fan of mythology."

"There's one simple reason these myths have endured the test of time," he said while placing his hand on the foot of Janus.

"There's truth in them," she answered.

"Yes, the symbol of one face looking back and one forward is powerful and, most importantly, true. I'm Janus. You're Janus. We are all Janus. However, I think most people miss the point of Janus. They focus on his face. They focus on either the past or the future, but Janus is here in the present. He is the god of doors. To me, he is the god of decision."

"Decision?"

"Let me ask you this question," the CEO said while walking to one of the doors. "If I could give you a time machine and let you travel to the past and talk with the Wright Brothers, would you?"

"Well, yes," she answered. "But I wouldn't go back and visit those boys with their flying machines. No, I'd rather go back and talk with Amelia Earhart or perhaps Coco Chanel or Marie Curie."

"Fair enough," he replied while mindfully noting that his collection needed a feminine perspective. "But if you traveled back in time and then returned to the present, you'd still be faced with the same decisions you had

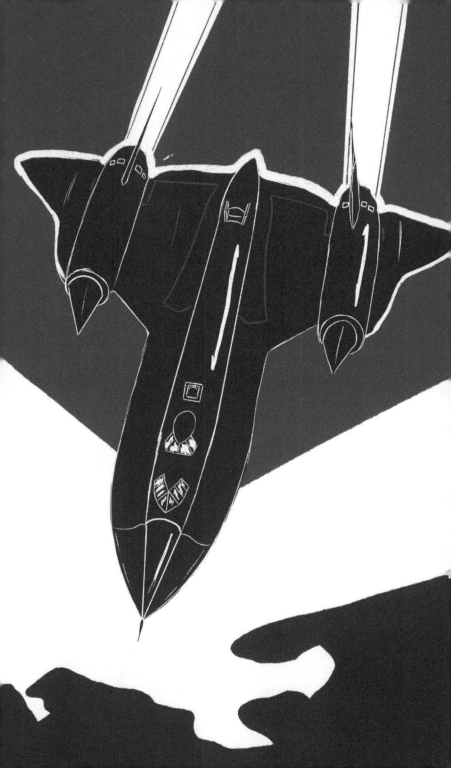

before you left. If you were, say, the CEO of Lockheed Martin…"

"Who is a woman," she interrupted.

The CEO smiled while picking up right where he left off. "If you were the CEO of Lockheed Martin, would going back in time and talking with Jack Northrup, Glenn Martin, Kelly Johnson or Ben Rich help you make the decisions you face today about the future of aviation?"

"Well, I don't think it would hurt," she answered.

"Yes, yes, of course, but we can walk right down that hallway and pick up Kelly Johnson's memoirs. And in those pages he talks about turning over the reigns of SkunkWorks to Ben Rich, and I can tell you exactly what he'd say to the CEO of Lockheed Martin today."

"Make a decision?"

"Yes," he responded. "That's it in a nutshell. Johnson was the guy who designed America's first fighter jet, the U2 and the SR-71 Blackbird. I mean, he was a legend. But, according to what Ben wrote in his own mcmoir *SkunkWorks*, Kelly Johnson called him into his office and told him two things in less than five minutes. First, 'be decisive'. He even told him that a 'timely wrong decision' is better than no decision at all. And second, he told Rich not to 'wound problems', but to 'kill them dead!'"

"Can I use that line sometime?"

The CEO nodded with a big grin, thinking of a few problems he'd like his talented COO to kill. However, returning to the subject at hand, he said, "no amount of time traveling back to the past is going to help you in the moment. There are serious decisions facing the CEO of Lockheed Martin today. What comes after the F-35, or will it be the last great American fighter? Is compact fusion real? Will the Hybrid Airship transform shipping and logistics? How will AI impact warfare? Will humans ever be out of the loop? How will you survive when the government finally admits it's broke?"

"And," the COO asked, "will an astronaut ever step foot on Mars?"

"More importantly," the CEO continued, "should we bet the future of the company on the Red Planet?"

"Should you ever bet the company on anything?" the COO questioned.

"Why yes," he responded. The best CEOs in the history of the world were always willing to make big bets with huge risks. It's the biggest and most important question any CEO like me, or like you, will face."

The COO began to feel the weight of the future on her shoulders.

"And will you be ready to make that decision? Will you have the courage to be decisive in those key moments and the thousands of small ones along the way?"

"Can you withstand the pressures of the present to preserve the future? And will you build an organization where everyone feels empowered to make the decisions necessary to our success?"

As the COO stood there in this strange space, thinking about her CEO's questions, she thought how different this discussion was compared to the class she took on strategic decision-making back in college. "One of my favorite CEOs once told me that a good decision—" as she remembered the professor lecturing with an air of haughtiness, "—is informed, timely, aligned with corporate priorities and scaled."

"Listen," the CEO said, "just as our lives are ultimately the sum total of the decisions we've made, the value of this business is the sum of its decisions. So, make a decision," he demanded while looking at the doors.

She knew what he was thinking. It was now her turn to pick a door.

The COO looked around for a second and quickly studied the doors. Each was a little different. One door was made of frosted glass with a black-and-white checkered pattern. Another, adorned with a brushed aluminum surface, was embossed with the image of a medieval knight. One door looked like it was made out of wood from a pier. Still another was bright red. And one featured a target on it. She was tempted to spend more time thinking about the meaning behind each door's design, but knowing this lesson was about being decisive in the present, the COO walked briskly across the room to the bright red door and grabbed the knob.

Inside, another door waited. Shutting the first door, she walked toward the second.

The CEO didn't follow her. Then, she opened the second door and looked inside. What she saw confirmed her initial thought that maybe she was in Las Vegas. Inside, the entire room was painted red, even the ceiling. In the middle of the room was a white card table with four white chairs. Sitting at the table were three men and a woman playing cards with a few people milling about. A few of them glanced at her.

"Poker," she asked?

One of the older men nodded.

Instantly curious to see what was behind the other doors, the COO excused herself and stepped back in through the vestibule. Once the door into the red room closed, she opened the door into the rotunda where the CEO was waiting.

"Do you play often?"

"To be honest, I prefer checkers," the CEO answered with a smile while glancing around at the other doors.

One by one, the COO stepped through each of these doors into a vestibule that acted, she thought, as a security system for the CEO's privacy and protection. On the other side of each vestibule was a series of, for lack of a better description, game rooms.

Behind the door with the checkered frosted glass were several old men playing checkers.

Behind the brushed aluminum surface embossed with the image of a medieval knight was a room full of men and women playing chess.

The wooden door that looked like it was made out of scraps from a pier included what looked like an intense game of Monopoly.

And the door that featured a target on it?

The COO walked through the vestibule into a digital shooting gallery that resembled a hi-tech arcade. There were classic arcade games like Space Invaders, Missile Command and Asteroids. There were modern games with giant curved screens. Twentysomething kids were playing Splinter Cell on an Xbox in the corner. And there were several pods featuring people wearing VR headsets and holding guns. As she looked around the arcade, the COO noticed one common theme. There were no Pac Man, Atari Super Sprint or other racing simulator games. No, every game was a shooting game. There was always a target and people were aiming and firing.

She was tempted to put on a VR headset and start shooting, but was more interested in getting back to the rotunda and the CEO. She knew the point of all of this and wanted to find out what was next.

Every room, every game, was about making decisions quickly. In a third-person shooter, you are constantly making decisions about which path to take, who to

shoot and when to pull the trigger. Monopoly involves decisions at every roll of the dice. To buy or not to buy? To deal or not to deal? Chess, Checkers, Poker, all games that require constant decision-making. Are you willing to sacrifice your Bishop or Knight in order to win? How many cards will you take? Is your opponent bluffing? Which defensive strategy will you employ? How much will you bet?

As she watched these young kids playing these games, she thought again about that long ago lecture on decision-making. "A good decision is informed, timely, aligned with corporate priorities and scaled." All true, she thought to herself, but why then do so many companies suck at making informed and timely decisions? Why do so many employees feel neutered, unable to make daily decisions critical to their organization's success? Why are reports written by Bain consultants about "The Five Steps to Better Decisions?"

Clearly, she could learn a lot by traveling back in time, but here in the present, it *is* about choices. Here in the present, it *is* about being decisive. The CEO, as usual, was right. Janus is the god of decisions.

As she walked back into the rotunda from the final door, she looked at the CEO and said plainly, "I'm ready to go to the future now."

With his protégé ready to journey into the future, the CEO gave one last look around the rotunda, pulled out his mobile device, and touched a button on the screen. As soon as he did, his COO heard all of the doors in the rotunda automatically lock with a loud click.

The CEO, who she knew was a little paranoid, looked at her and shrugged. "You can't be too careful when it comes to security."

Then, the statue of the Roman god Janus started moving.

<u>Chills raced up her spine as the statue rotated</u> <u>clockwise to reveal an elevator.</u> She couldn't believe it. For a second, she actually allowed herself to believe the rumors that maybe, just maybe, the CEO really did have a time machine.

The Chief Executive Officer stepped into the elevator and turned back toward his second-in-command. "If you come with me on this journey, I need to know you're all in. The CEO of this company, my company, must always see into the future. There will be no going back if you come down here with me. What you will see might shock you. It will certainly surprise you. I know it will challenge your ethics as you wrestle with its implications. It might even make you angry. But, there's no going back. If you really want to travel to the future, if you really want to lead this company into the future, I need to know you are committed. If not, you can leave right now, continue as my Chief Operating Officer or perhaps take the money you've earned and travel the world. And please know you'd always be welcome to come here and play checkers with me."

She smiled, nodded and then stepped forward into the elevator.

The CEO stepped in front of her and she saw something in his eyes she'd never seen before.

"I'm serious."

"So am I."

"You may not like what I've built down there. No one knows what I do."

She looked at him, not doubting for a second that what she would see would surprise her, but she trusted him, and had given all she had to both him and the company he had built. She had no choice but total commitment.

"I'm in."

The CEO moved aside to let her on the elevator and pushed another button on his mobile device and slowly the elevator starting moving down.

As the elevator lowered and its doors opened, the room came into focus. All she wanted to do was point at things like a little kid and ask, "what's that? What's that? What's that?"

The elevator came down in the corner of a room, with angled walls, baffles in the ceiling and what looked like acoustical tiling everywhere. It was also dark. While the rotunda was bright, polished and straight out of a Vegas casino, this room looked like a cross between a garage and a sound studio. The floor was carpet. The room was completely symmetrical. The angled walls and baffles on one side matched the angled walls and baffles on the other.

There was an empty table against one wall with storage underneath. Another wall was lined with shelves full of equipment, spare parts and more wires. It literally looked like the CEO had raided his own IT department for electronic supplies.

The third wall featured a giant floor-to-ceiling white board full of what looked like notes and formulas for product ideas. It even featured a rolling ladder so that whoever was using it could reach the highest parts of the white board while brainstorming. A modernist couch and a few chairs were casually positioned in front of the white board.

However, the white board, the shelving and the steel table didn't intrigue her as much as what was sitting right in the middle of the room.

"Is that, um, it? Is that the time machine?" She stuttered through the words, not believing she was actually saying them. The CEO though, was quick to respond.

"Yes, that's my time machine."

"Seriously?"

"Seriously."

"No really?"

"Really."

"Can we go anywhere?"

"Well," the CEO said, "that's the thing about time travel, you actually don't really need to go as far as you might think to see the future."

For a moment she doubted, as she thought his answer was a bit qualified.

And again, in this odd and stressful moment, she said exactly what was on her mind. "Is this just a gimmick?"

"Well, I wouldn't have invested millions of dollars in a gimmick. We will travel to the future in this time machine, but probably not in the way you are expecting."

"You mean I won't be able to see what Windows 20 looks like?"

"Honestly, do you really want to see what Windows 20 looks like?"

"Well, no, not really, but I'd love to travel two years into the future and see how our investment in…"

The CEO interruped her as he stepped toward his time machine. "But you see," the CEO replied, "that's the problem with time travel."

The COO followed him as he kept talking.

"It's really everyone's problem when it comes to seeing the future. People just can't look past the present. Everyone has a filter that's impossible to shake. I have a filter. You have a filter. We all have these limitations that hold us back from really seeing what the future can be. The truth is, the only way to invent the future is to go there and then look back. It's a matter of perspective. Too many people stand in the present and try to imagine what the future might be like. But without standing in the future and looking back, you can't get pass what I like to call the giggle test."

"The giggle test?"

"People who are standing in the present, or stuck in the past, they giggle at big, innovative ideas. They mock concepts they don't understand. Their creativity and imagination is limited by their perspective."

"Oh, no. I just giggled at an idea the other day."

"I know."

"What do you mean, you know?"

"This machine helps me, and will help you, stand in the future and look back."

"What do you mean, you know?"

"Why don't I tell you about this machine."

The CEO was now standing next to a small pod that looked like a cockpit. However, there was no stick or steering wheel. It featured a chair that looked like it was designed by the bastard love child of Charlotte Perriand and Arne Jacobsen.

A beautiful multi-screen dashboard wrapped around the chair. The COO moved closer and noticed a few speakers built into the chair along with some subwoofers in its base. Looking around the room, she now saw other speakers embedded into the angled walls and ceiling. She realized she stood in a room with the acoustics to rival a recording studio.

"I've spent years perfecting my time machine," the CEO said as his words now seemed so clear to her ears.

She stepped closer to the time machine, she was both fascinated and disappointed. She could clearly see that she wouldn't be flying anywhere across the space-time continuum, but at the same time, she knew this machine was part of a very expensive investment by the CEO.

"I'm a little confused," she confessed.

"Have a seat," the CEO said.

As she slid into the chair, the CEO pointed out a few controls on the dashboard. "You'll find the controls are quite intuitive. Just think of this as the world's most amazing boom box."

"What?"

"You know, a boom box," the CEO said.

"I know what a boom box is," she answered. "I'm just confused as to why you'd spend millions of dollars on a time machine that you could buy for $5 at a pawn shop."

"Well," the CEO chuckled, "I think you'll understand in a minute.

"As you know," the CEO said, "I'm considered a bit of a nut when it comes to acoustics and the audio visual systems in our conference rooms."

This, she knew, was true. The CEO was considered oddly obsessed with the design of the company's conference rooms and meeting spaces throughout its headquarters and sprawling corporate empire. Every meeting room featured a special acoustics package along with incredible microphones, speakers, video conferencing and other technology.

While most companies are satisfied with a starfish-shaped Polycom conference phone in the middle of the room, that just would not do for this CEO. She had actually seen the numbers. Like any good COO, she had questioned the money invested in these meeting spaces. The CFO and his minions in real estate and facilities had tried to drastically cut the A/V budget countless times.

When pressed, the CEO would always respond the same way, "I want my people to be able to hear each

other and be heard."

To most, it was just one more of the CEO's eccentricities.

This was a man who was also obsessed about keeping his company's secrets. The corporate headquarters had a security system as impressive as a Las Vegas casino. There were cameras everywhere. Everything was recorded. Executives could even request transcripts of meetings from a special intellectual property department within the company.

While this was something that everyone knew about because every employee, vendor and visitor signed a plethora of releases when visiting, no one really thought about it much. Sure, it kept people on their best behavior because they knew every word was being recorded, but mostly they were like reality television stars who simply forgot they were being recorded. The cameras simply vanished into the architecture of the building.

And besides, it was helpful to simply request a transcript of a meeting. At the end of the day, everyone knew the CEO was a bit strange. His paranoia was well-publicized and simply part of the corporate culture.

Now, as she sat in his so-called time machine inside a room with near perfect acoustics, she was starting to understand, but not yet comprehend, his obsession. She was starting to see that his obsession with security and acoustics were connected.

"What no one in this company knows," the CEO continued, "is why I'm so obsessed. Honestly, I'm not really worried about our competitors stealing our ideas. Most of 'em wouldn't even know what to do with our ideas in the first place. No, I'm worried about us missing something."

"Missing something," she asked?

"Yes," he exclaimed while beginning to pace around the time machine and preach as if he was pitching a new idea. "That's what I'm paranoid about. That's what I'm obsessed with! I am so afraid our company won't recognize a brilliant idea that will change the future. No, I'm worried about *missing* the future!"

"History is replete with examples of companies failing to recognize the future when it was right there all the time. Some idiot at *The Kansas City Star* fired Walt Disney as a cartoonist. A cartoonist! The newspaper editor said the Disney kid 'lacked imagination and had no good ideas'. And then, like 75 years later, another idiot inside Disney's own animation studio fired a young John Lasseter for pushing digital animation. Disney then, years later, had to buy Pixar for $7.4 billion."

Stopping for a moment to make his point, the CEO raised his hands while literally screaming "7.4 BILLION!"

Now circling the time machine again like prey, the CEO continued. "You have to ask yourself, how much would it have cost Disney to simply give Lasseter the

freedom to explore his dream of digital animation within the studio? Do you see what I'm saying? Thomas Edison was 20-years-old when Western Union fired him for experimenting while at work. And you know that I know your story. It was your first job out of college as an industrial designer for General Motors. It was your dream job. Any design major would die to work for a big car company. And you got fired! Fired by a middle manager for, what did he say in your performance review..?"

"Failing to conform to established design parameters," she said without hesitation.

"You were the future of General Motors," the CEO proclaimed. "You were the future, and they missed it! If a leader in any company wants to travel to the future, all he, or she, has to do is go listen to what people, younger people mostly, are talking about!"

"So," she asked, "is that what this machine is about?"

"Yeah," he said while affectionately patting the modern frame lining the dashboard. "A corporation, by its very nature conspires against the future. Senior executives, like you and I, can too often become islands of ignorance. Middle managers who are required to drive processes across a large organization can squash ideas without realizing their impact. Presentations by innovative employees can be politicized or positioned to the point of obsolescence. Occasionally, even an old-timer preaching fresh ideas is locked away as an individual contributor working

on 'special projects', but we all know what that really means, don't we?"

"But you are great, seriously great, with our employees, especially the young ones," the COO interjected.

"Sure, I work hard to be accessible. I walk the halls. I occasionally show up at meetings, but there's always this damn CEO filter. Fear, awkwardness and the inevitable crunch of time can get in the way. And, honestly, one of the reasons I'm 'great' with employees is because of the head start my little time machine gives me."

"Head start?"

"I think it's time for you to travel to the future," the CEO said while leaning forward and calling up a graphical interface on the dashboard. "Now, let's see what the program has for us this morning."

"The program?"

"Thanks to speech recognition software, artificial intelligence and an amazing algorithm developed by an old friend of mine, I can sit here and dial up any conversation."

"So," the COO whispered, "you were listening when I giggled."

"Well, I wasn't eavesdropping, per se," the CEO replied. "At least not live."

Desi

As the COO sat there with her jaw wide open, the CEO pulled up a list on the dashboard, in alphabetical order, of the basic departments and functions within his company:

- Brand
- Communications
- Customer Service
- Design
- Engineering
- Finance
- Government Relations
- Human Resources
- Information Technology
- Legal
- Logistics
- Manufacturing
- Product Management
- Research & Development
- Sales

"Well," the COO said, "you know me, I love *design*." And with that, she touched Design on the dashboard. Immediately, the screen revealed another list dating the meetings and a brief headline pulled from the program.

- 13 Days Old: Prototype for Project Pegasus
- 10 Days Old: Weekly Design Review
- 07 Days Old: New ID Lab Plan Presentation
- 02 Days Old: Concept Presentation & Brainstorm

"Um, let's go to the concept presentation and brainstorm," said the COO as she touched the screen.

In an instant, she began hearing voices all around her as if she was sitting in the presentation. Straight ahead, she heard the voice of a young designer facilitating a brainstorm. To her left, she could hear one of the design directors. To her right, the CTO. Behind her, a few more young designers.

"It's like I'm there."

"It's a time machine," the CEO said with a wide grin.

"You can add the video at any time, but I prefer to listen, as it allows me to focus."

The design director started talking about the objectives for the meeting.

"And this?" the COO asked while pointing to a digital wheel on the dashboard.

"With that wheel," the CEO confirmed, "you can fast forward, rewind or go wherever you want to go within the conversation."

Now the young designer at the front of the room was presenting an idea.

"Oh, this is wrong," the COO said as she pushed pause.

"Is it?"

"It's kind of creepy and Orwellian, don't you think?"

"Well, I agree that no one can know about this," the CEO replied, "but that's only because if people knew I was listening, they would change. They'd hold back. They'd constantly be positioning and politicizing. I want the unfiltered truth. I want to travel to the future by listening to our youngest employees pitch their ideas."

With that, the CEO leaned forward and pushed play.

"That sounds an awful lot like science fiction," the design director said.

However, he was cut off by the COO pushing pause again.

"Now," the CEO said sternly, "I really want to hear what this competent, professional and efficient middle manager thinks is science fiction."

"I get that," the COO said, "but it just feels wrong to be listening."

"No, what's wrong is missing an idea that will cost us billions five years from now. What's wrong is not finding those young and incredibly talented people who truly are the future."

"I guess, but…"

"But nothing," the CEO countered. "Do you know how I was able to pluck you out of the industrial design lab? Do you know why I have a reputation for being able to spot talent?"

The COO looked at the time machine in front of her.

"Without this time machine, I wouldn't be able to travel to the future by hearing what our youngest employees are saying. You have no idea how much I've invested in time and resources on the algorithm driving my little time machine. The acoustics in each conference room, the recording system, the voice-to-text, that was all pretty easy, but the AI and algorithm that literally listens to thousands and thousands of hours of conversations to find those important moments, well now, *that* is what makes this time machine special."

The COO clearly agreed with her boss, but she felt torn by the implications of what was, essentially, the world's most advanced spying machine. Inside her mind, a debate raged.

Was it really a spying machine if every employee knew that every meeting was recorded? Yes, but they don't know they are being recorded as part of a grand experiment by the CEO. Every employee knows that they can request transcripts through their executive. Every employee knows this! But they don't know the CEO has built an elaborate algorithm that analyzes every conversation. They signed a release. We pay them well. The intellectual property generated in these meetings belongs to the company and we can do with this data whatever we want.

Sensing this debate, the CEO leaned forward and asked her a question quietly while motioning to the dashboard. "Don't you want to hear what the design director thinks is science fiction? I know he's a very effective and process driven manager, but aren't you curious to see what he is about to kill with his giggles?"

At this point, the COO looked at her mentor's eyes, looked around the room and then looked down at the dashboard. She was astounded at the lengths the CEO had gone to build his time machine.

"If you think about it," the COO said, "there really isn't that much of a difference between reading transcripts from a meeting and listening to them."

"Exactly," the CEO replied!

The COO then reached forward and pushed play.

The End

Geoff is Founder & Chief Creative Officer of Creative Principals, a firm providing creative leadership for brand experiences, corporate visitor centers, museums and theme parks. Zoe is a designer and illustrator at Creative Principals as well as a costume designer for one of the largest dance wear companies in the world.

CPSIA information can be obtained
at www.ICGtesting.com
Printed in the USA
LVHW020727230420
653633LV00001B/1

9 780996 750479